AuthorHouse™
1663 Liberty Drive
Bloomington, IN 47403
www.authorhouse.com
Phone: 1-800-839-8640

© 2013 Students of St. Francis Xavier College, London. All Rights Reserved.

No part of this book may be reproduced, stored in a retrieval system,
or transmitted by any means without the written permission of the author.

Published by AuthorHouse 03/09/2013

ISBN: 978-1-4817-8664-5 (sc)
978-1-4817-8665-2 (e)

Any people depicted in stock imagery provided by Thinkstock are models,
and such images are being used for illustrative purposes only.
Certain stock imagery © Thinkstock.

This book is printed on acid-free paper.

Because of the dynamic nature of the Internet, any web addresses or links contained in this
book may have changed since publication and may no longer be valid. The views expressed
in this work are solely those of the author and do not necessarily reflect the views of
the publisher, and the publisher hereby disclaims any responsibility for them.

Every Day's a Holiday

Students of St. Francis Xavier College, London

It was Christmas morning

Johnny loved his presents so much. He was very happy.

Grandma gave Johnny his final present

'I wonder what toy this is' said Johnny as he opened the present

The present was a beautiful quilt with 8 squares.

'This isn't a toy' gasped Johnny looking puzzled.

'No' replied Grandma, 'but it is a very special quilt. It's a magic quilt. When you touch a square we will magically see lots of people having fun and celebrating.'

Johnny touched a square to see what might happen and

WHOOSH!

Suddenly Johnny and his Grandma were in an entirely different place.

'What's that noise' asked Johnny.

'Bagpipes' replied Grandma 'and it looks like we're in Scotland. I think we're about to countdown to midnight'

'Why would we do that'

'Well its New Year's Eve and when the clock strikes twelve it will be a brand new year. This is the Hogmanay celebrations'

10,9,8 .....

'Its so exciting' said Johnny and they both joined in the countdown.

5,4,3,2,1, HAPPY NEW YEAR.

There were fireworks and music and everyone was having a great time.

'We'll need to leave now Johnny as it will get very loud'

'I'll just press another square on the quilt.' Johnny pushed the square and

WHOOSH!

'It's a massive red dinosaur' yelled Johnny.

'No no, it's a red dragon but it's not a real one. It's made from paper and cardboard. Look at all the people carrying it.'

'Wow, and look at the red lights'

'Those are paper lanterns. Everyone is celebrating Chinese New Year!'

'But we've just seen New Year in Scotland, Grandma'

'That's right, but the Chinese celebrate New Year at a different time in January or February. Isn't it wonderful'

Johnny was really enjoying himself and then remembered there were more squares to press on the quilt.

'Oh I can't wait to see where we go next'

WHOOSH!

Everything suddenly appeared to be very green! There was a huge parade and everyone was having a wonderful time.

'It looks like we've landed at St Patrick's Day Johnny'

'Look at the funny costumes Grandma'

'They are very funny. They're dressed up like leprechauns. St Patrick is the Patron Saint of Ireland and Irish people from all around the world really know how to party on St Patrick's Day!'

'I really like the dancers' said Johnny.

'That is Irish dancing Johnny. It's very popular. The music is wonderful'

Johnny thought it would be a great idea to join in the dancing. He let go of Grandma's hand …. But accidently hit another square …. and we all know what happens then!

WHOOSH!

'I didn't mean to do that but look at all these lights Grandma,' said Johnny

'Aren't they beautiful. I think this is Diwali and it is a Hindu festival. The Hindus call it the Festival of Lights and that is why they light all these candles.'

'Are the boy and girl Hindus?'

'Yes and they live in a large country called India. This festival lasts for five days. Families celebrate together, wear brand new clothes and eat lots of sweets.'

As Grandma looked at Johnny she could see that he had discovered the sweets.

'The festival normally occurs in October or November. I think you've had enough sweets for one day Johnny. I'm going to push the next square.'

'I'll just have one more sweet' but as Johnny went to get more sweets ....

WHOOSH!

'I didn't get another sweet!' said Johnny

There were a couple of boys in front of a beautiful candle holder.

'Grandma, look at that. One, two, three, four, five, six, seven, eight, nine candles'

'This is another Festival of Lights Johnny but this time we are in a Jewish home. The festival is called Hanukkah and the candle holder is called a Menorah.'

'Do they light the candles all at once?'

'What a great question Johnny. They light the middle candle first and then for eight nights in a row they light the other eight candles, one at a time.'

'Look at the hats they are wearing Grandma.'

'Those are called Kippah and the boys wear them when they say their prayers.'

It was very peaceful and quiet. Grandma touched another square.

WHOOSH!

'Grandma' screamed Johnny holding on to her hand. 'Look at those ghosts and monsters.'

'There's nothing to be scared of' laughed Grandma. 'Behind those masks are little boys and girls just like you. Do you know why the boys and girls are having so much fun?'

'They have lots of sweets!'

'Yes they do. This is Halloween. The boys and girls are given the sweets when they go trick or treating. Everyone gets a treat' said Grandma, hopefully.

'Can I get a mask and go trick or treating at Halloween?'

'Yes you can but I don't think you should have any more sweets today' said Grandma.

'I think I'd like to be a werewolf'

'Oh that's very scary. I can't wait to see you in your costume.'

WHOOSH!

Suddenly Grandma and Johnny could see a family tucking into a big dinner.

'We're back to Christmas Day Grandma.'

'I don't think we are Johnny. I think we're in the United States of America and its Thanksgiving. American families have turkeys on Thanksgiving so it looks like a Christmas dinner. A man called Abraham Lincoln who was the President proclaimed a national Thanksgiving Day to be held every November.'

'I'm getting hungry' said Johnny

'So am I Johnny. We'll be home soon but isn't it nice to be thankful for everything we've got. You are a very lucky boy. Some boys and girls around the world have very little food and they certainly don't have a magic quilt!'

'There's only one square left. Let's push it together.'

WHOOSH!

'It's another feast,' said Johnny 'and look at those sweets! I really am very hungry now.'

'This is Eid Johnny and it's a very important day for Muslims around the world. They have all been fasting for a whole month that they call Ramadan and now they can celebrate and eat whatever they want.'

'I like that idea' said Johnny, getting hungrier by the minute.

'One of the traditions on this day is that they give as much to charity as possible so that everyone can enjoy a celebration and a nice dinner.'

'I really want my Christmas dinner now Grandma.'

'Well I think if we hold the quilt and just count down from five, four, three, two, one …

WHOOSH!

Johnny and Grandma were home.

There was a wonderful smell of Christmas dinner in the air.

'What was your favourite present Johnny?' asked Grandma

'It was definitely the magic quilt Grandma and this has been the best Christmas I have ever had.'

Johnny and Grandma sat down to have their Christmas dinner and told mummy and daddy all about the holidays and celebrations they had seen from all around the world.

CPSIA information can be obtained
at www.ICGtesting.com
Printed in the USA
LVIC051506180413
329846LV00003B